Snake's

Written by Sharon Fear

Illustrated by Geoff Cook

Snake slithered up to Rat.

2

"It's time for lunch," said Snake.
"And you are it."

Snake opened his mouth wide.

"What a big mouth you have!"
said Rat.

"Why, thank you," said Snake.
He was quite proud
of his big mouth.

5

"But it's not big enough to swallow me," said Rat.

6

"What!" cried Snake.
"I can swallow things
twice your size!
Three times your size!
Five times your size!"

7

"This is twice my size," said Rat.
"Can you swallow this?"

8

Snake took the ear of corn
in his mouth.
He gulped and gulped
it down.

"This is three times my size,"
said Rat.
"Can you swallow this?"

Snake took the cabbage
in his mouth.
He gulped and gulped
and gulped it down.

"Not bad," said Rat.
"But this is five times my size.
Can you swallow THIS?"

Snake looked at the pumpkin.
He opened his mouth wide.
He gulped and gulped.
He gulped and gulped
and gulped.

He swallowed it!

"Now it's your turn," said Snake.
He tried to slither after Rat,
but he couldn't move!
He was too round and heavy.

"Sorry I can't stay for lunch,"
said Rat.

"Never mind," said Snake.
"I couldn't eat another thing."